SCOOBY-DOO!

ANIMAL Jokes!

by Michael Dahl
illustrated by Scott Jeralds

Starring...

SCOOBY-DOO!

Shaggy! Velma!

Fred! Daphne!

...and more!

Raintree is an imprint of Capstone Global Library Limited, a company incorporated in England and Wales having its registered office at 7 Pilgrim Street, London, EC4V 6LB – Registered company number: 6695582

www.raintree.co.uk
myorders@raintree.co.uk

CAPG34359

Edited by James Benefield and Eliza Leahy
Designed by Bob Lentz
Original illustrations © Hanna-Barbera 2015
Illustrated by Scott Jeralds
Production by Gene Bentdahl
Printed in China by Nordica
0914/CA21401580

ISBN 978-1-4062-9239-8 (paperback)
18 17 16 15 14
10 9 8 7 6 5 4 3 2 1

British Library Cataloguing in Publication Data
A full catalogue record for this book is available from the British Library.

Acknowledgements
Every effort has been made to contact copyright holders of material reproduced in this book. Any omissions will be rectified in subsequent printings if notice is given to the publisher.

Set List:

What time is it when you see six chickens outside?
Easy, it's six a-cluck!

What happened when the cow ran into the barbed wire fence?
***Udder* destruction!**

When did the pony answer the teacher's questions?

Whinny had to!

What did the horse say when it fell?
"Help! I can't giddy-up!"

What do you give a pig that has a sunburn?

Oinkment!

How does a cowboy keep track of his cattle?
He uses a cow-culator!

Why did the sheepdog keep walking along the road?
It didn't see the ewe turn!

Who is a chicken's favourite composer?
Bach! Bach! Bach!

What do you call a really cold cow?
An Eski-moo!

Who's the cow with the sunglasses
and the drumsticks?

He's a moosician.

Where do cows go if they're tired of eating grass?
A calf-ateria!

Where do most horses live?
In a *neigh*-bourhood!

What did the chickens do when they lost the football match?
They cried fowl!

Why do cows lie down in the rain?

To keep each udder dry.

What do you call the hair on a cow's upper lip?
A moostache.

Does anyone know where those lost cows are?

Nobody's herd.

A pig, a cow and a chicken held up a bank. How did they get caught?

The pig squealed!

What did the chicken say after it laid a square egg?

"Ouch!"

Why did the calf cross the road?
To get to the udder side!

Have you heard about the farmer who thought
he was a goat?

He'd felt that way ever since he was a kid!

How did the sick pig get to the hospital?
In the ham-bulance.

Why do chicken farmers do so well at school?

They're always egg-selling!

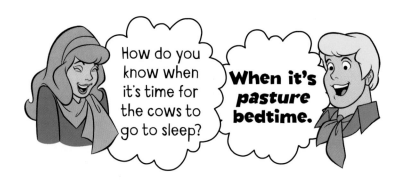

How do you know when it's time for the cows to go to sleep?

When it's *pasture* bedtime.

Have you heard about the farmer who needed more room for his pigs?

He built a sty-scraper!

Have you heard about the farmer who drove his cows on a bumpy road?

He wanted a milk shake!

Have you heard about the farmer who crossed a cow with an octopus?

He got an animal that milked itself!

I don't think this cow has any milk.
Well, try the udder one!

Do you know that scientists think they have discovered bones on the Moon?

Jinkies! Sounds like the cow didn't make it!

Bit two:
Out of the blue

How did the lobster cross the sea?
It moved from tide to tide.

Have you heard about the man who thought he was
an electric eel?
It was shocking!

Where do dolphins come from?
Finland.

Why do sharks swim in salt water?
Because pepper makes them sneeze!

What do you call photos of a piranha?
Tooth-pics!

When do ducks wake up?
At the *quack* of dawn!

VELMA: Did you know that whales are very musical creatures?

SHAGGY: Really? I suppose that's why they play in orca-stras!

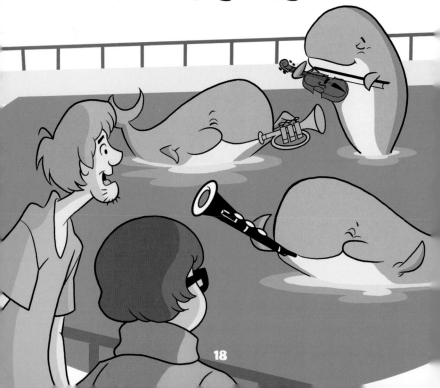

What's the best time to buy canaries?
When they're going "cheep"!

Have you heard about the duck who didn't go "Quack" but went "Moo" instead?
Sounds as though it was learning a "moo" language.

Where does a squid keep its wallet?
In an octopurse.

What did the snail sitting on top of the turtle say?
"Slow doooownn!!!!!"

What do you call a duck that eats gunpowder?
A firequacker!

What do you get if you cross Cinderella with a fish?
Glass flippers!

What do you call a bird that's out of breath?
A puffin.

What kind of bird will steal soap from the bath?
A robber duck!

Where does an octopus like to relax?

In an arm-arm-arm-arm-arm-arm-arm-arm chair!

Bit three:
Man's best friend (and other pets)

What kind of dog loves bubble baths?
A shampoodle!

Where do bunnies go if they're sick?
The hop-ital.

What do you call a cheerful bunny?
A hop-timist!

Why did the bunny stop jumping?
It was un-hoppy.

What did you do when you caught Scooby eating the dictionary?

I took the **words right out of his mouth!**

Have you heard about the mother cat that swallowed a ball of wool?
Yeah, she had mittens!

Where do cat lovers go on holiday?
Purrrr-u!

Why did the rabbit go to the bank?
It needed to *burrow* some money!

Is it easy to buy cat food?

Yes, you can get it purr can!

VELMA: What's Shaggy doing out in the garden with a shovel?
FRED: Cleaning up the Scooby-Doo-doo!

FRED: What do you call little dogs that like to visit the library, Scoob?

SCOOBY: Uh, hush puppies?

Why did the rabbit go to the barber?
It was having a bad hare day!

What do you get if you cross a frog and a dog?
A croaker spaniel!

What did Scooby say when he
sat on sandpaper?

Ruff!

Bit four:
What do you call...

... a fish with no eyes?
Fsh.

... a bear with no ears?
B.

... a fly without wings?
A walk.

... a bird on an aeroplane?
Lazy.

... a lamb with no legs or head?
A jumper!

... who has scratches all over his face?
Claude.

... who carries her pet tortoise wherever she goes?
Shelly.

... whose dog always makes holes in the garden?
Doug.

... who loves to touch all the animals in the
pet shop?
Pat.

... who keeps bees?
Buzz.

... whose pet camel doesn't have any humps?
Humphrey.

... who put his right hand in a lion's mouth?
Lefty!

How do you scare away bugs?
Call a SWAT team!

What do termites do when they want to relax?
They take a coffee table break!

How do fleas travel from dog to dog?
They itch-hike!

What does the queen bee do when she burps?
She issues a royal pardon!

What insect flies, drinks blood and talks in code?
A Morse-quito!

Why was the firefly sad?
Because her kids weren't very bright!

What did one flea say to the other?
"Shall we walk or take the dog?"

Name the fastest insect in the world.
The quicket!

Why did the two termites stop drilling through the floor?

I give up.

They said it was really boring!

How many insects does it take to fill a flat?

Ten ants!

What did the termite say when he walked into the saloon?

"Is the bar tender here?"

How do you find where a flea has bitten you?

Start from scratch!

What do little bees like to chew?
Bumble gum.

What's a mosquito's favourite sport?
Skin-diving!

What has antlers and sucks blood?

A moose-quito!

What are just-married spiders called?
Newly webs!

What did the mother worm say to her son when he came home late?
"Where in earth have you been?"

What happened when Scooby chased the monkey
with a stick of dynamite?
It went BABOOM!

What kind of bear is always wet?
A drizzly bear!

Have you heard the joke about the skunk trapped in
the Mystery Machine?
Never mind. It stinks.

Why was the frog sent home from school?
It was hopper-active!

What did Shaggy say to Fred when they were hiding from the tyrannosaurus rex?
"Doyouthinkhesaurus?"

How do elks send messages to each other?
Moose code.

What's Scooby's favourite snack at the zoo?
Chocolate chimp cookies!

Why do you never see a camel
in the jungle?
Because they're so good at camel-flage!

What language do polar bears speak?
North Polish.

What happened when the chameleon walked over the feather?

It was tickled pink!

Why did the monkey always wear shoes?

So he didn't have bear feet!

Why did the leopard wear a stripy jumper?
So it wouldn't get spotted!

Why did the crocodile cough?
It had a frog in its throat!

What do you call monkeys that are best friends?
Prime-mates!

Why aren't elephants very good dancers?
Because they have two left feet.

What is a llama's favourite drink?
Llama-nade!

What is big, muddy, has tough skin, and can put people into a trance?
A hypno-potamus!

What is a polar bear's favourite meal?
Ice bergers.

What kind of clothes do kangaroos wear?
Jumpsuits!

What kind of shoes do frogs wear?
Open toad!

What do you call a baby hippo that still wears nappies?
A hippo-potty-mess!

What do you call a lion that eats your mum's sister?
An aunt-eater!

Which snakes are the best at maths?
Adders.

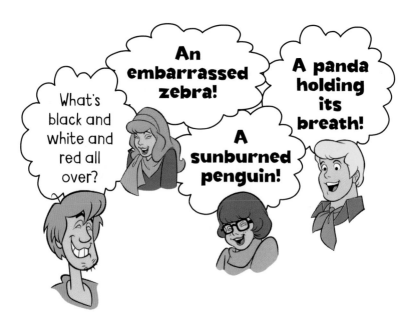

What's black and white and red all over?

An embarrassed zebra!

A panda holding its breath!

A sunburned penguin!

What is big and grey and grey and
grey and grey?

An elephant stuck in
a revolving door.

What do you call a gorilla that has bananas
growing out of each ear?

**Anything you want.
It can't hear you!**

What is a python's favourite game?
Swallow the leader!

Is it hard to spot a leopard?
No, they come that way.

What kind of music do bunnies like?
Hip-hop!

What does a mother snake do if her baby
snake has a cold?
Viper nose!

Do you know
how to make an
elephant stew?

Yep. Just
keep it
waiting for
an hour!

How many skunks fit in the Mystery Machine?

Quite a phew!

What did the boa constrictor say to the monkey?
"I've got a *crush* on you!"

Scientists have discovered the bones of a prehistoric pig.
They're calling it Jurassic Pork!

What do you call a cobra with no clothes on?

Snaked!

What did one toad say to the other?

"Warts new with you?"

What do you call a baby kangaroo that stays indoors?

A *pouch* potato!

What's light and fluffy and swings from trees?
A meringue-utan!

What do you get if you cross an alligator with a bank robber?

A crook-odile!

What did the judge say to the skunk?
"Odour in the court!"

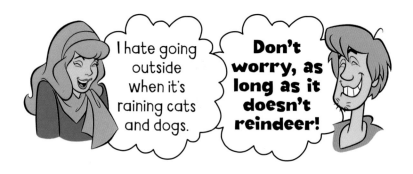

I hate going outside when it's raining cats and dogs.

Don't worry, as long as it doesn't reindeer!

What did the leopard say after dinner?
"That sure hit the spots!"

What did the scale say when the elephant tried to step on it?
"No weigh!"

What kind of animal has white fur, lives in the North Pole and likes to ride horses?
A polo bear!

What do you give an elephant that feels sick?

Plenty of room!

How to Tell Jokes!

1. KNOW the joke

Make sure you remember the whole joke before you tell it. This sounds obvious, but most of us know someone who says, "Oh, this is so funny..." Then, when they tell the joke, they can't remember the end. And that's the whole point of a joke – its punchline.

2. SPEAK CLEARLY

Don't mumble: don't speak too quickly or too slowly. Just speak like you normally do. You don't have to use a different voice or accent or sound like someone else. (UNLESS that's part of the joke!)

3. LOOK at your audience

Good eye contact with your listeners will grab their attention.

4. DON'T WORRY about gestures or how to stand or sit

when you tell your joke. Remember, telling a joke is basically talking.

5. DON'T LAUGH at your own joke

Yeah, yeah, I know some comedians crack up while they're acting in a sketch or telling a story, but the best rule to follow is not to laugh. If you start to laugh, you might lose the rhythm of your joke or stop yourself from telling the joke clearly. Let your audience laugh. That's their job. Your job is to be the funny one.

6. THE PUNCHLINE is the most important part of the joke

It's the climax, the reward, the main event. A good joke can sound even better if you pause for just a second or two before you deliver the punchline. That tiny pause will make your audience mentally sit up and hold their breath, eager to hear what's coming next.

7. The SETUP is the second most important part of a joke

That's basically everything you say before you get to the punchline. And that's why you need to be as clear as you can (see 2 on the opposite page) so that when you finally reach the punchline, it makes sense!

8. YOU CAN GET FUNNIER

It's easy. Watch other comedians. Listen to other people tell a joke or story. Go and see a good comedy show or film. You can pick up some skills simply by seeing how others get their comedy across. You will absorb it! And soon it will come naturally.

9. Last, but not least, telling a joke is all about TIMING

That means not only getting the biggest impact for your joke, waiting for the right time, giving that extra pause before the punchline – but it also means knowing when NOT to tell a joke. When you're among friends, you can tell when they'd like to hear something funny. But in an unfamiliar setting, get a "sense of the room" first. Are people having a good time? Or is it a more serious event? A joke has the most funny power when it's told in the right setting.

How is **Michael Dahl** different from a mousetrap?
One is full of tales, and the other is full of tails!

Dahl has created more than two hundred tales (not tails) for young readers. He is the author of *The Everything Kids' Joke Book*, *Laff-O-Tronic Joke Books*, the scintillating *Duck Goes Potty*, and two humorous mystery series: Finnegan Zwake and Hocus Pocus Hotel. He has toured the United States with an improv troupe and began his auspicious comic career in primary school when his stand-up routine made his music teacher laugh so hard she fell off her chair. She is not available for comment.

How is **Scott Jeralds** like a stampeding rhino?
They're both smash hits!

Not only is Jeralds a smash hit, but he has created many a smash hit, working in animation for companies including Marvel Studios, Hanna-Barbera Studios, M.G.M. Animation, Warner Bros. and Porchlight Entertainment. Scott has worked on TV series such as *The Flintstones*, *Yogi Bear*, *Scooby-Doo*, *The Jetsons*, *Krypto the Superdog*, *Tom and Jerry*, *The Pink Panther*, *Superman*, *Secret Saturdays* and he directed the cartoon series *Freakazoid*, for which he won an Emmy Award. In addition, Scott has designed cartoon-related merchandise, licensing art and artwork for several comic and children's book publications.

Joke Dictionary!

bit section of a comedy routine

comedian entertainer who makes people laugh

headliner last comedian to perform in a show

improvisation performance that hasn't been planned: "improv" for short

lineup list of people who are going to perform in a show

one-liner short joke or funny remark

open mike event at which anyone can use the microphone to perform for the audience

punchline words at the end of a joke that make it funny or surprising

shtick repetitive, comic performance or routine

segue sentence or phrase that leads from one joke or routine to another

stand-up comedian who performs while standing alone on stage

timing use of rhythm and tempo to make a joke funnier

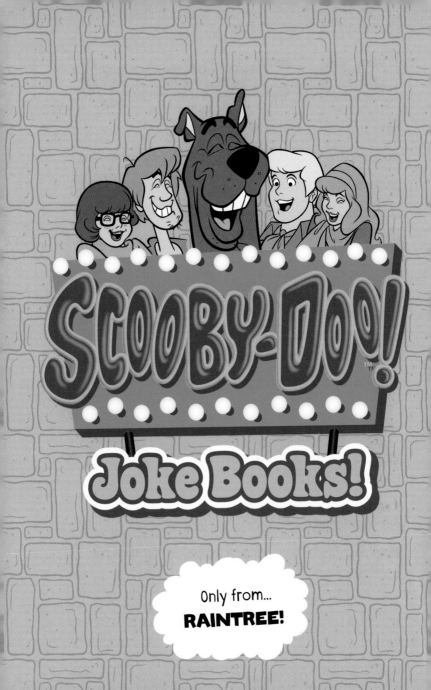

SCOOBY-DOO!

Joke Books!

Only from...
RAINTREE!